THE 100 POETRIES

SHAYNA ARORA

ISBN 979-888569181-9

Contents

Contents

Contents

Contents

The opinions / contents expressed in the book are solo of the authors and do not represent the opinions / standings /thoughts of compiler/ publisher. this book has been published with all reasonable efforts taken to make the material error-free after the consent of the author .No part of this book shall be used or reproduced in any manner whatsoever without written permission from the author , except in the case of brief quotation avoided in critical article and reviews the author of this book is a solely responsible and liable for its content including but not limited to the views, representation, description , statements, information , opinions and reference.

The content of this book shall not constitute or be construed or Deemed to reflect the opinion or expression of the publisher or editor. Neither the publisher nor editor endorse or approve the content of this book or guarantee the reliability ,accuracy or completeness of the content published herein and do not make any representations or warranties of any kind, express or implied, including but not limited to the implied warranties of merchantability, fitness for a particular purpose. the publisher and editor shall not be liable whatsoever for any errors , omissions, whether such errors or omission result from negligence , accident , or any other cause or claims for loss or damages of any kind , including without limitation , indirect or consequential loss or damage arising out of use , inability to use , or about the reliability , accuracy or sufficiency of the information contained in this book.

Acknowledgements

The making of this anthology would not have been possible without the writer . thanks to everyone who has worked hard and has made efforts for this book to be a success. above all we thank almighty God for giving us opportunity and strength to complete this book successfully .
We are thankful to quidditch ink publication without whom this project wouldn't have been possible.
lastly ,we thank our family and friends for supporting us thoughout this .

Disclaimer

This anthology is fiction .

the writer has tried to do her best and made plagiarism free.

In case of any plagiarism detected ,

neither the writer ,

nor the publishers are responsible .

Preface

The 100 poetries contain poetries written at different times and prompted by very different feelings .

In my book I discuss both my experience and love toward words .

This book have scribbled down the words in such a way that you'll live , feel and will fall in love with the words and feelings hidden inside them .

The books motive is to ignite love and happiness in the society and create a sense of this appearance of their sorrow.

I being the writer of "THE 100 POETRIES " Hoping that you'll find amazing poetries in my book that I hope will touch your heart

.

About The Publication

The Quidditch Ink Publication is a publishing community house of The Inkzoid foundation. It was founded in 2021 by Nilanjana Sarkar. The publication who recognizes the talent of the youths, to contribute themselves in the field of literature. We help them to bring together and to unite across the nations, to publish their creativity for the upgrade generation. Think for the future, work with the experience from the past, action it on the present and be consistent.

This will take you with the simplified approach of publishing your books. We would be happy to receive your manuscripts and

meeting talented authors and co-authors on board.

We would love to deal with your beautiful poetries, mictorals, stories, and other write-ups. Here we will put dedication and efforts to become more environmentally friendly and will encourage authors to move forward in life.

We will provide you with a writer's congenial platform which will enhance the smooth working of our cell and the relations too.

Our work will always provide you with the finest quality

We will offer you the most affordable packages with exciting offers. Which will be fully customizable.

We especially Pride ourselves on the strong relationships we have with both authors and all literary agents .these important elements are why we consistently manage to publish such a high -quality and popular books

Contact us to find out more :-

Instagram :- thequidditchink_

About The Founder

Nilanjana sarkar

Author Nilanjana Sarkar Hails from West Bengal, alipurduar and currently she is studying in class 12th and worked as an head of the publication in WYIMUN on based on the three committee WHO, UNHRC and UNDP .she is the founder of the the Quidditch ink Publication , she has also worked as an entrepreneur with Team Elite which deal with E- commerce ,direct selling and social media platforms ,she has already completed her internship in marketing by UNLEASH YOUR PASSION ,she has been awarded as Dada Saheb Phalke award and extra ordinary talent award on 2020 by star and genius book of record, forever star book of record as an achiever of the year and warrior of change 2021 from award Arc, her article had also get published and features over realpreneur.com, entrepreneur ethics ,India ethics maxstern media ato links dailyhunt, the weekly mail, and yourstartup.in as a celebrity author ,she is very hardworking and passionate girl and loves to do creativity through her writing ,she mostly rights on erotics stuff as well as on many topics which helps her to explore the more and more she is public speaker as well as motivational speaker she is and impulsive writer who oozes out her emotions and feelings and thoughts by writing join her on Instagram

_nilanjanaaa

About The Writer

In this chaotic world she is the serenity you will crave for . most probably shayna Arora hails from the city of "food basket sriganganagar", Rajasthan.

She is from hindu family but believes in humanity .

She is a student and pursuing her graduation in humanities (English hons.)

She love to express her feelings through writing because she feels that pen and paper are hers best friend .

So, she worked in many anthologies and her self book got published named "MERE KRISHNA" available on amazon and now she giving her best to this book "THE 100 POETRIES "and expect for the best .

1. if I die young,

Know if I die young,
I will be sorry for the disappointment,
Sorry for breaking your hearts,
Sorry for welcoming your tears too early,
Sorry for the deep sorrow in your souls,
But wasn't my will; it had to be done.

Please if I die young,
Remember the seasons we had under sun,
Remember the fun that made us cry,
Remember the joy that came with tears,
Remember all my goodbyes I had said,
Let the memories of today be your sorrows.

My friends; if I die young,
Read my work louder than before,
Sing my songs more than birds,
Spread the words day by day,
Be scared not of the copyright,
You will be my successors.

My sisters; if I die young,
Hold your hands to fill the gap left,
Remember my name in your souls,
Remember the jokes that brought fights,
Remember the life we shared from young age,
Say goodbye to them all forever.

Dear parents; if I die young,
I thank you for your care and love,
Forgive me for wasting your investment,
Forgive me for fearing to stay for a while,
Never blame yourselves for my travel,
Blame my soul instead for getting tired.

Oh, my lover; sorry for leaving too soon,
Sorry for the breakup that came unwilling,
Please clear my messages to free yourself,
Send away good memories with my bad deeds,
Knowing that I didn't love you,
That's why I left you too soon.

Remember this please; if I die young,
Dress me in white with red tie,
Let my final bed be full of roses,
Lower me ten feet instead of six,
Send me away with love songs,
Lord will make you a rainbow to shine upon you all.

In memory of all young individuals who lost their lives during the COVID-19 pandemic.

2. POWER OF GENTS

Gentlemen say hi,
Raise your voices hit your chests in pride,
For your powers are the most valued,
I give you a five-star appreciation,
For you play a big role as heroes,
Let the world salute at you gents,
Take the respect,
As you build a great world for all living,
Power at work implies love at heart,
Give your protections,
Secure all you care of,
As security is your concern all through,
Spit love and caring words,
Kidnap their heart on love web,
As affection is what you give at best.

3. A POEM ABOUT FATHER

You have been like that canopy of tree in whose shade we rest.
Doing all the hard works and sacrifices alone to offer us the best.
Teaching us how to never complain and deal with lives' evil test.
And always backing us up whenever we get troubled and stressed.
I know except on father's day, you are not appreciated enough.
A mother shows her love daily by caring and affectionate touch.
But you choose to love us silently without expressing it much.
So may be we could not love you back as much as you deserve.
For all your selfless deeds without expecting anything in return.
As of course we can not ever repay for whatever you have done.
What best we can do is to try to be a proud daughter and son.
And be capable enough to tell you to ease as now it is our turn.

4. LADIES IN THE HOUSE

Beautiful, wonderful, cute ladies,
Hear my voice; I say hi,
You're one of a kind,
With high price tag I guess,
With filters or not,
Black, chocolate or brown,
I only call you my cutie dear.

Wish had the power to sail down the ladder,
Calling and cheering to each one of you,
Right from Deborah's smile,
Blending with Scar's sweet voice,
Not walking past Hellen's love and kindness,
Down the road rejoicing with Joy,
At last, resting my case on Darlene's comfort zone,
But too bad the book can't hold the ink's weight.

I make my way,
Feel the warmth of the house,
Stay supreme and prime,
Because you are worthy it.

Chapter5

जिंदगी एक झूठ हौ झूठ हैै, सपने सभी,।

मैं भी झूठा, तुम भी झूठे, झूठा हैै हर आदमी !!

रिश्ते झूठे, नाते झूठे, झूठे हैै अरमान भी,.!!

इस झूठ को सच मान कर, खुश हैै देखो इंसान भी,

देखो, सच पक रहा हैै, इन झूठो के आँच पे,

फिर क्यों अंधेरे में जी रहे हो, सारी सच जान के,

सच कहो खुश हो क्या तुम,

इस झूठ के संसार में,

आखरि क्यों खरीदी,

ऐसी जिंदगी जो मिली उधार में,

मेरी मानो मत चलो तुम, इन झूठे राह पे.!!

देखो सच सामने है,

स्वागत के लिए द्वार पे...:)

6. ABORTION

Hey there, I wanna be that clear,
Please open your ear and hear,
Abortion is a crime depending to its time,
Sorry for who I condemn, but fact is always prime,

Why kill an infant ready to live?
Why destroy your product before arrive?
Why to love make a dive,
When you know at last abortion will drive?

Can't you hear the cry in you,
Or your heart is that dark instead of blue?
When injections you take, tablets you chew,
Sticking to your decision with glue,

It may be an accident but why risk?
For your life, death to whisk,
Girl, please open your eyes today,
Boy, please avoid the betray,

I rest my case, I give you the space,
But know the unborn is full of grace,
In future will be the one to embrace,
Please let it see your face.

7. A GRADE

She was an intelligent girl,
She enjoyed learning new things,
So you wanted her to excel in studies,
Stating that this would result in her good being.

She toiled hard to be the best,
As you were never satisfied by her grades,
You replaced her toys, drawings
And novels with heavy books,
Ceasing the joy of her childhood days.

She grew up as a bookworm,
Who studied all day long,
So everyone expected her to be smart,
And her answers to be never wrong.

Soon she was exhausted,
Hiding behind perfect student mask,
and her grades started to deplete,
Her health was ailing,
But her poor academic performance
Is what you could see.

She was stressed about your expectations,
And that she couldn't be the best again,
But you failed to realise
That the A+ in her marksheet
Couldn't heal her slit vein.

8. LITTLE GIRL

As the little girl I was, learning to be proud and strong,
Growing up to be a perfect someone who does no wrong,
Head filled with sad songs, not knowing where do I belong,
False hopes and dreams of the future bottled me up all night long.

Time flows like the stars, feet soon decorated with scars,
A heartfelt confidence, an unlimited freedom on oneself,
I used to be a child of high expectations on myself,
Now everything has changed before I even knew,
As staring back at the mirror and question; who are you?

Hours turned to years have passed and it's a mess,
An endless of greed and ambition increase to impress,
And the friends I had drifted apart one by one,
Lonely without the loved ones, ecstasy was close to none,
I closed my teary eyes to the present that couldn't be altered,
But that's alright, just live life to the fullest, and that's all ever
matters.

9. NATURE'S PLAY

Nature is happy watching today's play,

Eyeball is turning into color grey.

Amazing sky is crazy, today earth is so lazy, Blowing air is pretending, sitting kingfisher is sucking candy.

Flowers are competing and also cheating, All animals are busy in helding their meeting.

Nature is happy watching today's play,

Eyeball is turning into color grey.

As soon music started rain start dancing, Further soil replied both are laughing.

Suddenly the clouds disappered from the sky, All butterflies decided to run above the fly.

Nature is happy watching today's play,

Eyeball is turning into color grey.

A person is sleeping on the pasture land, Unforgettable is this marvellous day. Nature is happy watching today's play,

Holding a loaf of bread in his right hand.

Gluttton man is unaware of today's play,

Eyeball is turning into color grey,

Nature is happy watching today's play, Eyeball is turning into color grey.

10. Just friends? Really?

She fell for him a very long time ago. Not for his looks but for his personality. She ignored all her feelings and tried to kill all her butterflies because deep down she knows he can never be with her. She doesn't deserve him. She ignored that feeling yet got attractions from many but the feeling which she used to get on his sight remained constant. Her feelings didn't fade away, they just got fainted. Years later they both are best friends. She pretended that she has turned her emotions button off but she still had those for him. Just she was not able to understand those signals

Just friends? Really?

Then she should not get that crazy smile on seeing his message; she wouldn't just keep spending the whole day thinking about him; she should not get jealous of his crush. Really? Just friends? Deep inside she knows it's something more than friendship.But she can't confess those feelings for him because she knows friendship is more important and he loves someone else.
Entire day she is a happy soul for him. He thinks he understands her like noone else . He cares for her. But he has no idea about the reality. He doesn't know that his best friend has been hiding her emotions since 4 years.
Every night she cries her heart out in hope only if he knew and

stayed awake. She found her feelings getting stronger and hard to confess day by day. She decided to write everything on a paper because she can't confess. But unfortunately,he caughts it up. He becomes dumbstruck after reading that. He couldn't expect this from his best friend. He can't believe that his bestie has been holding so many emotions from so long. He lefts shockingly.She cries, because this is nothing less than a breakup for her.He didn't turned up for few days. He kept thinking about the whole thing. He loved someone else but many questions popped in his head. Why does the whole thing bothered him? Why did he cared for her? Why she matters for him a lot? Because he too loves her but he realised lately. And yes it was really late because her bestie was not able to bear that pain and passed away through heartbreak.

He lost the moon while counting the stars....

कुछ बातें हैं तुमसे कहने को अगर मैं कहूँ तो तुम मान लोगे क्या?

मैं कहूँ अगर कि मैं सोयी नहीं कब से रात भर तुम्हारा इंतज़ार करती हूँ तो तुम मान लोगे क्या?

कुछ पल के लिए ही मिलते हैं हम फिर हर लम्हा तुम्हें याद करती हूँ तो तुम मान लोगे क्या?

मैं कहूँ कि दुनिया भर के सामने मैं हमेशा मुस्कुराती हूँ मगर मेरे आँसू सर्फ़ तुम्हारे लिए बहते हैं तो तुम मान लोगे क्या?

यूँ तो बातें बहुत कम होती हैं हमारी मगर मैं कहूँ कि अपना दिल खोल कर मैं सर्फ़ तुम्हारे सामने रखती हूँ तो तुम मान लोगे क्या?

12. IF MY PEN ENDS

What will happen if my pen ends?
Will my name be erased?
Will my work be forgotten?
Or I will be the news's title?

If tomorrow my pen is no more,
What will be the title to my story?
That I was great,
Or I was a passerby in this jangle?

I'm in fear if my pen comes to an end,
What will I become?
What will my work become?
Or I will end too as the pen?

It is a great debate inside me,
Debate that is full of fear,
As I watch my pen drain out,
What will happen next?

13. IT'S OVER

Lord where did I go wrong?
This road being too long,
I never heard this before but now it came,
Striking hard and harder like wrestling game,
I can't believe that it's over,
Instead of your face; your back you turnover,
My words for apology never heard,
Sticking to a dark face which you didn't had,
If this is the way, I better die,
I'm tired of painting dye,
For others to enjoy the beauty and sweetness,
Lord you are my witness,
Love is blind, truly it is,
Harshly stepping on you with no peace,
Even when you think you are in love,
It turn out that you're left in half,
I try not to hate myself,
But the faith place me on that shelf
I try not to cry,
But that is the only will,
I don't know how to say goodbye,
And I don't feel the word to come by,
If you gonna walk, go for better,
If you going to stay, stay forever,
The year it's over,
The trust is over

Love no more our cover,
Thank you for saying; it's over.

14. SOMEONE I LOVE

He thinks I don't, but I do,
I know he loves me more than I do,
But I do care of him more than he thinks,
Love is one big fight,
Good or bad can be put into write,
Never pressure your soul to stress,
I will always try to impress,
Focus and see,
A drop of ink in a sea,
That is my love in my silence
I love you more than you can sense.

15. TEAR

Every drop of my tear reflects in night,
By bright and sharp rays of moon,

Thousands of secrets float in it,
Make it heavy to shed from eyes,

The clouds in me are craving to cry,
But every storm hides their cries,

The rain in them is similar to tears,
I want to collect but everyone dies,

I am not eternal to cry for ages,
I am a stupid fallen for wise.

16. SINNER

God built me too much comfort in life and said you are a sinner
to feel the misery of reckless pain
after all I was a fool,
I preached his comfort,
All to evolve in life
But I evolved as a sinner
And ,
I died as a sinner at the end,
Because comfort within me never grew to define peace and love
nor
to catch me up with the pattern of what life held,
Rather I saw everything as war within humanity,
I saw people's voices raising towards what's wrong than right
It was hard for me to build comfort from within every day and
night,
I fell through the heights--
Heights Where People burnt me inside their minds,
Saying that I don't know misery of pain,
And there I was living inside of myself,
Laying In the graveyard of sinster.

17. Lies

People are full of lies,
And so am I,
As I choose to live in a beautiful dilemma
Each time I lie.

I lie everytime I say I'm fine,
Coz no one really cares even if I'm lying.
There hides a lie in every it's okay,
Coz no one tries to find what's wrong
And what am I hiding.

There is a lie behind I don't care,
Even when I know how much it hurts,
Or maybe I'm not lying,
Just choosing among the truths,
That hides behind these words

18. SHAM HOTI GAYI

Sham Hoti Gayi Suraj Dhalta Gaya,

Main Musafir Tha Main Chalta Gaya,

Ek Ek Karke Mujhse Har Shaksh Door Gaya,

Jis Jis ka Mujhse Matlab Nikal Gaya.

Jin Logo Ko Main Apna Aaina Kehta Tha,

Waqt Ke Sath Wo Aaina Bhi Badal Gaya,

Kuch Patthro Se Thokar Bhi Khayi Maine,

Un Patharo Se To Main Sambhalta Gaya,

Har Ek Rishta Mutthi Me Ret Ki Tarah Tha,

Jo Dhire Dhire Hath Se Fisalta Gaya,

Sham Hoti Gayi Suraj Dhalta Gaya,

Main Musafir Tha Main Chalta Gaya.!!

19. Night Sea

It's so dark,
So cold, and empty.
The waves crashing and thunders humming,
From far away,
Earth trembled and shook.
The darkness engulfed from each crook.
The lightning made way,
A sudden ray of taunting hope.
Across the wide ocean,
Light shone from above,
Into the depth of the dark void,
Nowhere to run and hide.
Unknown creatures slipped in turmoil.
Feel so small, at the center of the vast sea,
So noisy but silence is all that lingers.
Thousand pairs of eyes watching from beneath,
A tremendous sight, a scary experience,
Standing alone in the middle of a monster.

Thrills and chills, swallowed in the darkness.

20. KISMISS BLOOM

It was Christmas eve,

She was about born

Dusk was at end when.,

She bloomed on earth

born to an angel

with glory and grace

Innocence spread her veins,

Patience invaded her mind,

Sorrows filled her heart.

16 hours passed,

The ocean rushed towards her,

Welcomed her with fierce power

leaving innocent corpse behind.

Sixteen miserable years passed

without beauty nor freedom

her talents were drowned in her tears

until the day came

she found her reflection..

She believed in the mighty above

The stars that shine at night;

The wind that touched her curls,

The sun that dried her tears;

And the one who lead her dream

21. AJIB SI..

मैं हूँ थोड़ी अजीब सी

मैं बादलों से डरती हूँ बरसात पर मैं मरती हूँ

जब हवाओं के संग उड़ती हूँ तब भी जमीं से जुड़ के चलती हूँ

हाँ, मैं हूँ थोड़ी अजीब सी, मगर प्यार सबसे करती हूँ

कभी सागर की चट्टान हूँ कभी रेत बन किनारों से जा मिलती हूँ

मैं इंद्रधनुष की बेला हूँ मैं हर घड़ी रंग बदलती हूँ

हाँ, मैं हूँ थोड़ी अजीब सी, मगर प्यार सबसे करती हूँ

जो बात मुझे सताए, मैं तंग उसी को करती हूँ

कल रूठ गयी थी जिस बात पर, आज पसंद उसी को करती हूँ

बिन कहे कुछ कहती हूँ, बिन सुने सब समझती हूँ

हाँ मैं हूँ थोड़ी अजीब सी, मगर प्यार सबसे करती हूँ

बात है बस इतनी सी, जो हर बार कहती हूँ

हाँ, मैं हूँ थोड़ी अजीब सी, मगर प्यार सबसे करती हूँ।

22. THROUGH THE DARK

The shore is covered by my trails
Hands covered with sand
Watch them white in beautiful lines
I would rather see this world through the Pearl on the sand
A million voices, silent dreams
Where hope is left so incomplete
My spirit talks, I know my soul believes
I would rather feel this world through the golden dream
Darker times will come and go
Times you need to see us smile
And home is warm and mild
I would rather feel this world through the Paint of our moments
When a human strokes your skin
That is when you let them in
Let them in before they go
I would rather feel alive with a dance in the rain
The hunter's moon is shining
I'm running with the wolves tonight
Please don't leave me here Row the boat take me home

23. NUMB...

Time has passed,
Like the smoke particles in the air,
Chaotic silence and painful grief that I'd to bear,
A demanding wish to forget the past,
And the memories of regrets that ripped me apart.

Time has passed,
Like the season of monsoon in a desert,
Feeling like dirt as I embraced my body in hurt,
Nothing to stare, pure sadness and empty rooms,
My eyes transfixed to an unknown distant,
An endless void, forcing my mind to feel paranoid.

Time has passed,
As the pain and anger numbed me over the years,
Never leaving me like the salt in the sea,
So I welcomed them with open arms,
An unbreakable bond as they became a part of my charms.

"Feelings are what help us grow. They're also what help us connect to people but the existence of numbness'll be there to break that connection."

24. DELUSIONAL HUMANITY

As life shows its light,
The human kind keeps to write,
In their mind and heart, you will be right,
All they spit is your genus, your bright,
To your start they will forever smile,
Your progress they will file,
And that is their style,
But all turn to a lie,
Today they will be friends,
Tomorrow destroy your dreams,
Maybe its to my community they are ghost,
But current humans, all has to come with cost,
Man, be strong never fear the hurt,
Do what you feel with all your heart,
Let the success build you a hut,
Its your life, their talk can't make any cut.

25. Waiting for Love

The sparkling bright lights turned into a sign of passing years,
Time flies by in a blink of an eye and it became a fear,
I'm here, still waiting for someone to appear,
Soothing me from my tears, arms around me from the shears.
On the valley with meadows full of roses and thorns,
I was in awe, admiring as the wind dried the raindrops on my face,
Heartbeat in race, mindset drifted off into deep space,
Even if I don't understand the complexity of love and happiness,
No reason to quit and still have to look for one.
As waiting for someone is like an addiction,
To become my life's permanent affection,
To bring out the blue skies after the rain in their will,
Only thing that I didn't realise you were there among the crowd,
How could I have not discovered that love was just beside me?

26. true love

One day,
When the sun no longer rise,
And moon loses its shine,
The time no longer in track,
The space cease to abstract,
I'll be on the other side,
Waiting for the moment to arrive,
For we to meet again,
Without farewell to come,
And when that time reaches us,
Be sure to look for me,
I'll be waiting for you,
Don't you forget me.

27. I AM SORRY

My eyes blinked hard
Breathe in too deep
Sweat poured so much
Mind blanked as white sheet
I turned around and searched
The melody of darkness around me
I cursed towards the emptiness
While i know the problem is in me
I shut my eyes to blind.
I cover my ears to deaf.
My legs are wobbly as I try to escape
My chest is stuck and out of breath
I feel so heavy and drained of strength
I fall everytime I lose my balance
I lost in the unconscious of painful despair
The lost parade that I pray to get
The losing games that I dared to play
I turned and betrayed the painful reality
And spent a fortune for a soothing fantasy
I deleted 'loyalty' from my life permanently
Last word from me is that, "I'm sorry.

28. Yet Still A Dream

Waking up while watching the sunrise,
As the sun kisses your tender skin,
Making sparkles in your beautiful eyes,
As the warmth envelopes o'er you,
As the sky illuminates the colour blue.

This is all but a dream now,
But I know one day it'll come around,
Where I'll be there with you,
Snuggling and hugging you like a cocoon.

29. Sea...

Sea...

Oh how beautiful

With you, the sunset is!

The view itself seems like an imagination.

Like an art of work from god himself.

Lost between thoughts and emotions that arise, here I stare,

With such amusement

Oh, how heavenly it feels,

With the slight breeze that touches my skin.

The smell of you,

Oh, how fond of it I am,

This beautiful view

You, the sunset, and I,

Oh, how I wish that this lasted forever.

So that I can put aside my hurting past,

And just stare at you, as you take down the sun.

The sun himself is powerful

But you, my dear,

Aren't you even mightier?

You, even though, look serene in this wonderful evening,

Here you are, gobbling up the sun in whole!

It seems so real, but is it?

Or are you a deceiver?

Just like her?

30. Locked Up Mind

If only there were things to recover,
I would take the memories and not the person,
Because the memories stay pure and sweet,
While humans are two-sided imps.
Rather than gambling my happiness,
I would take the easy route,
Without risks and worries, I'll live
And hope for a better tomorrow.
It's the destiny I chose,
The journey I walked into,
And I wouldn't change my mind
For some uncertain promises.

31. Sometimes I forget

Sometimes I forget,
That I have blood in my veins, not liquid fire.
It's tears rolling down my cheeks, not rivers.
It's a heart in my chest, not a glacier of ice.
I really forget, as if I have drunk from the lethe.

32. Emotion

I never felt this for a long time,
I was stupefied.
I might as well be reckless,
To hold this emotion up high.
But it's what keeping me alive;
The thing that keeps making my heart beats,
That I can feel the adrenaline rush,
And blood flows faster than it should be,
Activating my nerves, as in the fight-or-flight.
Surfing through my veins, and lightened up my brain.
I never thought to have feel this before,
You give me hope and light,
Oh now, how could i meet you
Without calling you 'mine'?

33. PASSING

Life is like a card game,

And now have gained fame,

We are staying today,

But tomorrow leave our way,

Right now, open is the eye,

Tomorrow our souls rest in the sky,

Now we are standing on the floor,

Next second we pass through the door,

Tomorrow has its own secret,

On it never dream to place a bet,

The grave is not satisfied,

Each day keeping us dried,

Taking those we love,

Leaving our hearts in half,

Staying with full pain from the burn,

Dying inside slowly with the shot from the gun,

Today you are present,

Tomorrow you are absent,

Hello sister and brother,

Wish you can find one to fix to another,

We don't know about tomorrow,

It may come full of sorrow,

Only what we can do is just praying,

That every tomorrow we remain staying.

34. Never be the same

You are in my head,
You are in my blood,
You are inmy veins,
You are in me forever,

Days without you feels dead,
Life without you seems hard,
Thoughts of you come in chains,
Being the same without you is never,

It's you beibe,
Who make my mind run insane,
Who make life never be the same,
Who runs through my veins,

Just know my apart is useless,
Because you went wrong with my brain,
And now can't even think straight,
I never be the same any more.

35. WITHOUT YOU

Wish I had ability to lie,
That I can stay peacefully after your bye,
I can enjoy my time without your hi,
But none of it can successfully apply,
Instead stay day by day making my cry,
As the sweet memories can't die,
Wishing your love again I can buy,
To fulfill our dream of going to Dubai,
Enjoying the beauty on your eye,
Truly without you around, life is like a fly,

36. I AM OK

Currently my soul has noticed the best,
No regret any more for loving you,
Lying to me that you were the best we take the journey,
But in the middle of nowhere throwing me out the vehicle,
Breaking my trust and love more than anything I thought,
But I say thanks for letting me know this and what you were made of,
For I am ok that ever,
My wound healed by someone who knows what is love,
Giving me all in brim even when I say it's enough,
And that is my match I needed all that time,
Just save your strength and walk your way,
I'm ok now, tomorrow and forever.

37. BE NOBODY'S DARLING

Eyes look like,
You Will dislike,
I want to enjoy alone,
Without burdens,
Calling everyone darling.
Freedom of my heart,
Start a breath without hold,
Not an image of someone,
To stick on my mind bold,
Be nobody's lover
Be pleased walking alone,
Be an outcast of your own,
Be nobody's darling,
Enjoy your life growing.
Be no one's abductor,
Be nobody's burden,
Just enjoy the feeling of unburden.
Why grow thin and weak?
Why spend days and week?
Thinking and dreaming of someone,
Who at last leave for the other's affection?
It's better I go for Java,
Than waste my time to be a lover,
Being in love is a task,
That drain your mind, finance even strength.

I rather be the poet of the sun,
Than waste my time playing on sand,
I rather walk away,
Than loss my way In love

38. LIVING IN FEAR

We are living in world of fear,
Fear of our own secrets,
Fear of our friends knowing about ourselves,
Fear of our families,
Fear of those we love,
Fear of our day-by-day enemies,
Fear of making the speech,
Fear of disclosing the truth,
Fear of each outcome on our deeds,
Fear of our own selves,
Fear of living on the own,
Fear of changing our lives,
Fear of making decisions,
Fear to face our fears.

39. WILL BE BACK SOON

I'm gone,
But remember my spirit is on,
Will be with you through my arts,
Let the poetry words fill your hearts,
It's just for a while,
I will be back to re-open my file,
Pray for me to be back,
Soon before the world turn dark

40. YET STILL A DREAM

Waking up while watching the sunrise,
As the sun kisses your tender skin,
Making sparkles in your beautiful eyes,
As the warmth envelopes o'er you,
As the sky illuminates the colour blue.

This is all but a dream now,
But I know one day it'll come around,
Where I'll be there with you,
Snuggling and hugging you like a cocoon

41. 30 DAYS OF LOVE

BE HONEST

If I showed you my dark side,
If I turn to be a fool,
If I loss what I have now,
Tell me honestly, would you still love me the same?

If my pen fades,
If I take a rest,
Would you still love my work?

Would you still cheer for me?
Would you still stand by me?
Would you still miss me?
Tell me honestly, would you?

42. SOMEONE

I found someone,
She calls me handsome,
I call her my Babie,
She just replies yes cutie,
It's just awesome,
Blessed with flat tammy,
Cute lovely hips,
Not yet old but around 20's
On her smile, what the golden lips,
Saying fish is the food crowned,
Dancing being her number one like,
Not into drugs but to chips,
Crushing life as a packet of Crips,
And that is someone I found,
Who I can settle with to the ground,
My heart forever she crowns,
As she twinkles more like a star,
My sweerie, sweetie I found.

43. HONEY

How deep do you thing I love you?
How sweet can you think this may be?
If I stand and sing the song high and low,
I love you more than you can love me.

I can't tell why I love you,
But can narrate how I cherish you,
For my heart can't lie before you,
As the feelings widely they woo.

You my hearts puzzle,
Lowered from heaven for my sake,
So, my soul you can nuzzle,
Loving you is not a mistake.

I can't explain how you beautiful,
I can't deny saying you wonderful,
You my baby love,
Who owns my half.

You sweet more than the pineapple,
You lovable like an apple,
You my one and only,
I love you today and forever.

44. I'M SORRY; SHINE MY VALENTINE

I'm not good in apology but this is my best I can try,
I meant when I said I love you today, tomorrow till I die,
For love jangle there are ups and downs that make us cry,
Please to my mistake never stick and say goodbye,
I hate myself too,
But I need you to be my valentine boo,
To shield my soul from love harm,
As I hold you close with my arm,
Saying yes, I am,
In love with you even when they cast any charm,
Please, hear my cry for once,
Give me one more chance,
Make the day and shine my valentine,
Let's put the worst and all mistake into one line,
Let's focus on the great and best for our love to be fine,
Forever I'm yours and you are mine,
And there I take the blame as I say I'm sorry,
Let's open new chapter, let's restart the story

45. HEARTACHE

Pain lies inside,
The feeling no more at hide,
Love isn't something to ride,
Nor blindly into, you slide,
Someone to call dear,
Is someone to create fear,

I have a heartache,
My whole night being awake,
No chance to have the break,
And this is the feedback of love being fake,
Even a glass of beer,
Can't change the gear,

I loved, respected even cared of you,
Only fooled by the phrase "yes I do"
Now no more my baby boo,
Stress, heartache and depression stuck on me like glue,
My death even coming near,
I hate myself for taking the spear.

46. LOVE

It said money can't buy love,
Neither can you gain it through shove,
For this is something precious,
Though not taken seriously will turn to be acrimonious,

Love is one thing to cherish,
As it can save a soul from perish,
Preventing any shed of blood,
Forever staying calm from war flood,

Love is one thing to fear,
For it can fill a tank with tear,
Bringing the end to two lovers; no more cheer,
Dwelling as enemies though used to call each other dear,

Love is one of the dirtiest games,
More when it generates a lot of blames,
Burning up more than a candle flame,
Later leaving you on an open shame,

Never hit your chest that you are in love,
For it may fall any time; I mean from above,
Love has no owner,
Only who knows is the donor,

47. HATE ME

Tell me how you came to hate me,
Explain to me why you dated me,
Tell me how it chanced to replace me,
Tell me how it came to be me,
I wanna know why you did this to me,
After time by time, you chased me,
Now you are an enemy to me,
I need to know why the knife felt on me,

Tell me why you hate me,
Tell me why other lover not me,
My mind needs to know, please help me,
I cherished you, why did you leave me?
Why take courage to do this to me?
Knowing I fear goodbyes but anyway say it to me,
Then erased me,
Wishing you never dated me.

48. GIVE ME A CALL

I don't know what to do,
I don't understand what is to be done,
Gave a promise to be around,
But let all fall to the ground,
Have tried my best,
Instead, my choice rest on nobody's chest,
Right now, I need you,
Please give me a call.

Never let me walk my way,
Leaving you is one crime to regret,
Just fight for the heart,
Let you soul be calm in my hut,
Never take long to notice,
Please give me a call.

49. SOMEDAY

When I was young, I had one project,
One mission and vision that had select,
The wrong to be put to correct,
Whole world as one to be connect,
Not yet but someday is what I expect,

I started my art with one goal,
Words of love and unity be spit by my soul,
Stay in people's heart as Davido, Justin and sauti sol,
My love be their love in whole,
Not yet but someday I will be fully in that role,

Stepped into relationship at teenage with on aim,
Trust, love, care and comfort I claim,
Though it turned to be my worst game,
Breaking and burning my heart as flame,
It's painful but someday I will reclaim,

I wake up every morning with one desire,
My future life be of great even when I retire,
All that I need by just a say I acquire,
Instead, day after day all grow high and higher,

Though I believe someday life will not be that hot as fire,

Time after time I wish people around me would see,
Even the blind to try to agree,
Project, goal, aim and desire are as important as degree,
All of them play as life key,
And someday, will bring an escort to your coffee or tea.

50. DEAR HEART

Why don't you lament over what you lost ?
Under dark clouds and month of May,

What has stopped you to ignore the cost?
Of gleeful days spent with her,

Everything is changing with breeze of life,
Why don't you forget the dreadful past,

What has kept you unchanged from years,
Amidst hearts that change everyday.

51. COMING HOME

It has been ups and downs,
Walking through floods and droughts,
Both freezing and melting out,
Now I'm coming home,

I'm tired of walking and running,
I'm tired of hiding and hunting,
No more struggles and surviving,
Now I'm coming home,

No more crying and fear,
But only support and care,
Neither more predators nor hunters,
As now I'm coming home.

52. DANCING WINDS

A riddle a day keeps you serene and sway,
Some believe the reality is real as they say.
With wonder, the consciousness they convey !
I don't doubt what they say is to obey,
A lonely globetrotter comes ruminating at the bay.

53. I bet for sure, this is a goodbye

I see through your fake smile,
I see light dimming in your eyes,
I see it all through your mind.

Your hands touch me with hate,
Your voice trembles with lies,
Your kisses harrass my mind.

Love is fading like sunset light,
Lifelessly I lie in your lap.
I see you loving someone new.

Pull the trigger right into my heart,
Let me bleed painlessly and die.
I'll say I'll heal and just smile.

I am wearing a mask of lies
But deep within I'm drowning
Trying to love what is not mine.

I bet it is time to accept my fate.
To let you go is something I hate.
Holding onto you is same as to die
And I bet for sure, this is a goodbye.

54. MIDNIGHT RIDDLE

If I tell you all about her, would you be wise to know who she is.
If I warn you about her, would you care to take my advice. Well riddle me this.
Men opt to drink down their sorrows because of her, some feel without her life is worthless. She goes with many companions, some have been called anger and jealousy. She can make a grown men feel young again.
"If I tell you about her, could you say who she is".
She is the cause of the death for many, kings leave their thrones for her and princes betray their land for her.
Women have felt her touch and dived into her arms, men saw her afar and craved for her presence. She is a glamorous flower at a distance and a thorny rose in close sight, she is a beautiful puppy from afar and yet a rabies infected dog nearer.
She is the reason men have killed women, it is in her name that heart were broken and crushed.
If I tell you about her, would you be able to depict her name.
Pastors preach about her,and families are built and destroyed in her name. Some grow in her and some fall in her......

[FOR THAT SPECIAL WOMEN IN YOUR LIFE]

55. DREAM

The conscious feeling,
In your deep unconscious mind,
Are the imaginations you see,
That were blessed to you from god.

The imaginations you see,
Is a preview of what your life could be,
Its like a message from god,
Telling you what you see can be.

Then these thoughts we sight were shared,
To the loved ones we cared,
For then these thoughts crashed in a swing,
Like a plane that had no wings.

They are loved ones which is true,
And yet cannot see what our hearts drew,
For the thoughts that were new,
Just dropped like a dew,

The realization we must seek,
Is that our imaginations is what we see,
For god has given it to me,
And not to anyone else indeed,

f the dreams you see needs to be killed,
Tell it to a person,
Whose mind is as small as a pill,

Though if the dream you seek needs to be done,
Work for it and pray with your heart,
For god will grant it,
Like shooting star.

56. ENTANGLED SOUL

My soul born free, is now hindered,
In the paths of this cruel world full of relationships,
responsibilities and duties.

Entangled in the burden of expectations,
Enangled in unwanted needs and greed,
Entangled in the shimmer of the wordly riches.

My soul is in despair,
Desperate to be free.
The negative enclosure crushes its emotions and even thoughts
too.

My soul yearns to be released,
To break free.
Free to breathe, free to live,
Yet again !!

57. Fed up with life

On the corner of the busy street
Hiding the sorrows behind a rigid face
A trembling hand begs
Begs for attention to earn a single cent
Belittled by the society
They bag their pride
Keeping it aside,
To carry on with dear life
Not much, but enough for a humble meal
A glorious day
Not for us, but for the trembling hand.
The sun rises, and it sets
Minutes seem to have no hurry.
The struggle to live,
Not a moment to relax
Not a second to enjoy
Should strive every minute
To get along with precious life.
A future of darkness
The present of diminished light.
Hopeless or nor
Not a soul to care.
The trembling hand,
Fed up with life
Spends such a dull life,

Until god invites.

58. LIFE

The more you experience it,
The more you know what life means.

When the aroma of the coffee goes perfectly with toast, it is life.

The happiness you feel when a
Baby smiles at you is life.

Finding your first love in the school corridor is life.

The smell of new books is life,
Rolling tears make up life.

The healing music is life,
Letting go of your past is life.

Sleepless nights, sweet dreams
And nightmares are life.

Feeling the warm sun,
Staring at the cold moon is life.

Spending time with friends and
Getting betrayed is life.

Being jealous is life,
Appreciating kindness is life.

Enclosing arms around you is life,
Tasting the taste is life.

Crying hard is life.
Smiling, laughing and enjoying is life.

59. TWISTED HEART

The winds blow and our words flow.

Our hearts beat and the birds tweet.

It is mystical indeed, how hearts meet,

And how we run into new souls as the days unfold.

One time, they're all green, yes a "stranger"

But bit by bit, our hearts and souls surrender.

And we regain composure.

Finally realizing that the "stranger" was not an intruder

But can rather be a sister, brother or even a lover...

With them, we find our laughter and our days are brighter.

Yes, everything seems far better as our pains become lesser.

And that was how I found you, but I still wonder,

If truly this can last forever...

Of course, I've met a million hearts in the past, but we're now asunder.

My mind vividly recalls all we encountered together,

And if I say it doesn't hurt, call me a liar.

But here I am, again a Dreamer.

Dreaming of a forever and having you in the picture..

Surprisingly, I don't seem to bother cause I have faith in Mother nature.

Oh yes, I'm it's creature and I believe it works in my favor.

For though I lose a million hearts, ten new more do I capture.

And I'm at ease, yes I prefer the ten rather.

Perhaps, they posses what I require to go higher.

And so, dear "stranger", I deem this a great honor.

For I careless about who you are or where you're from, as long as you're a true lover.

Join me lets stroll on this pasture and not be mindful of where it's takes us.

All I know is, at this moment you're my anchor despite the raging clutter...

60. Broken Heart

Emptiness took away the
words from my mouth.
My hands still tremble,
My pen is scared to write.

A thought of her name,
I think not twice.
My brain goes numb, memories
Flash before my eyes.

I'd say I'm strong,
But my tears, I can't hide.
I'd say I'm healing but
That won't make it right.

Promises, broken.
Cuddles, forgotten.
Calls, missed.
How fast time flies!

Our precious love
That once moved mountains
Is now just a fantasy
and a dreamy night.

61. THE HEAVENLY PORTAL

There was a war going on in the chambers of my heart,
Foreign to the result, I decided to play My part.

I went to the terrace to discover myself amidst the chaos,
As I had lost myself while wandering in the corridors of eros.

Up above, I found a thing to share my lonesome sight,
And it promised to stay with me until every fortnight.

*When I gazed into it, I got enamoured and beguiled by its beauty
soon,*
*A wraith silver disc hanging in the lonely sky and oh! I found My
Mr Moon.*

I discovered something beautiful about the moon that night,
*While it gently twirled the darkness of my spirit into a blissful
light.*

When I felt the gentle touch of the moonlight all over my skin,
For a moment, I felt the battle inside me has entered into its

coffin.

*I acknowledged the magic in my bones as the Moon mumbled in
my ears,
The heavenly portal has opened to spill blessings to choke all my
fears.*

62. MISSING HEART

mug of blood for my heart,
to survive after her depart.
although veins and arteries are apart,
my soul and my heart is one part.

diamonds are found in dirt!
brightest stars shine in the dark,
kind souls are left hurt!
and in my heart there is a mark

my soul's is numb,
fingers are cold,
I'm dumb,
it's hard to hold.

my blood froze,
veins are dead,
missing my rose,
coloured in red.

my legs are not moving,
can't see cause my eyes are swollen,
among the dead but still living,
but I can feel the memories that aren't stolen.

voice of hers, sweet as honey,
worth a lot of money,
without you, there's nothing funny,
it's raining but also sunny.

my heart left her sweet scent,
i can follow and find where she went,
letter of mine was sent,
sad as it can be! I'm going to lament.

i wrote your name in the clouds,
but my breath blew it away,
i wrote your name in the sand,
but my tears washed it away.

i wrote your name in my heart,
and you became mine.
I'm missing you and it hurts,
but you are worth the wait, so it's fine.

63. Love...

The word itself seems so vague.
A curse: A cure: by many names it is known.
It all seems nothing in the eye, who failed at love,
But in the other, it seems divine.
When god created such a feeling, was it meant to be released to
the world of humans? Or vice versa?
Was it meant to have two sides?
The side that cuts your heart like a poison knife,
And the other which heals you like a heavenly medicine.
Was it for the happiness of beings who strive for happiness?
Or was it for them to suffer more?
Love, for some is happiness and for some it's a curse...
And who is the decider of who gets what?
Is it god? Is it fate?
Or does it depend on oneself?
So many questions, yet to be answered
Can we incriminate god for keeping us in such a dark?
Or should we grind to find the light ourselves?
Was god so incogitant or was it all for us to discover?
All these questions burn within
Someone who waits a hopeless wait
To have a go once more
At the love that they lost.

64. A MORNING RAG

Someone has been tuning my spine,

All night with guitar-pick nails,
Seemingly dreaming of Fernando Sor,
Performing for the fallen of Pigalle,
For whom he composed 12 Pagan Waltzes.

On the bright side,

Her face is less swollen than the moon
And she imbibes my offerings of juice
Mouthing logical inconsistencies
Creatively enough to warrant a forever.

BY SANDHYA

65. IF ONLY

If only you'd hear my heart break, you'd see the pain of my love for you.

If words written in ink could have the expression and emotions of the heart, perhaps you'd know men are the same but do things differently.

If love was written in the eyes I have, you'd see a different love than the one painted in movies.

I fear the change that comes with tomorrow, for it will eradicate the moment and feelings of today.

I'd be nice if tomorrow never came and we could live in today forever.

66. BLEEDING SHADOW

Devoid of stars
Is my night sky.
Filled with pain,
My scars cry.

The darkness blows
Its mournful bassoon.
Before my eyes
This blood red moon.

I never knew you
Would depart this way.
You were the Sun
That brightened my day.

Walking together on
The edge of doom.
I think I lost you
Way too soon.

I'm sure I won't make
It without you.
Everything just reminds
Me about you.

How you used to smile
Like sunshine in the rain.
How your love soothed me
In the worst of my pains.

But all I'm left with is
This bloody moon.
It daunts me just like
A beast of the doom.

I see myself bleeding,
All of my hope fading.
But take your time as
I would still be waiting...

67. A LETTER FROM THE SKY

If somehow all your plaintive pleas
don't reach my ears tomorrow,
if all sweet dreams you dreamt of me
take shape of grief and sorrow.

If somehow all get crush on you
and they get on their knees,
and you find all pleasures, false or true
but get no more of me.

I wish so much you would not cry
with your nerves so pale and gray,
nor to life you would say goodbye
and slay yourself that way.

For I wish so much to see you live
to see you smile all day,
to discern the love I could not give
before I went away.

So fear no more these worldly sorrows
nor awful twisted words,
rather hear me calling every morrow
with the blended notes of birds.

Feel my touch so calm and soothing
in the warmth of summery sun,
catch my fragrance, strong and pleasing
when the frantic day is done.

And remember one day far from crowd
where the blue sky meets the land,
I'll be waiting for you, all unbowed
to greet and kiss your hands.

68. Oh! This beauty

Oh! This beauty unbound,
I'm trying to fill it into my mind and soul.

No words can describe it.
No lens can capture it.
It is beyond one's imagination.

Nothing can pull me back from this
Gushing wind and the rushing water.
It is much calmer than my screaming selfish world.

My soul bows in a gratitude undefined.
O! Almighty Creator of unparalled blessings,
Your world is undoubtedly better than my world.

I can't thank you enough for pulling my soul away from this
harsh world often to realise this priceless beauty.

69. we both

I danced on smooth ice and my feet were bare.
You played with fire until there was no more flames to spare.

You who were always grateful for the sun and the stars,

Your smile has drooped, things have changed.

We both have burnt, but with a different flare.

70. HIS PRESENCE

Ever so careful, ever so tender he started to tend to me. I watched him being so focused, I watched his gleaming green eyes, his short black bangs, his soft brownish skin, his lips....

But what I was grateful for was none of that, I was grateful for one thing only

HIS PRESENCE

71. LAST TIME

Oh my stars, last time I cried to you, that this is the end.

Last time, I told you these wounds are impossible to mend.

Last time, your cool breeze caressed my warm tears. Strength to me you tried to lend.

And last time, you whispered back, "the wounds will be scars, my child, it's not the end."

72. CAPTIVATED

Amaze me with your words,
Like that time you insulted me,
Warm me with your embrace,
Like how you had choked me,
I'll forever stay, so don't you walk away,
I'm held captive, but you dare think to escape?

Desperate and devastated,
I roll in disgust.
You made me like this,
Who are you to judge?

73. The Place You Created

I believe, somewhere
some far away,
There must be a place,
You've created unintentionally.
Like how you thought the clouds were candies,
And the lakes, oh so soft,
Like chocolate cream.
The trees were lollipops,
The sand was butter sweet.
I believe somewhere,
some far away,
A place I'd like to visit, and stay the week.
A place you created for our friendship's sake.
A place we created to fulfil our dreams.

74. Talking to you

Talking to you felt soft,
As if I'm on clouds,
Puffy,
but transparent.
Flying through the wind,
Not too fast, as if I'm just floating by,
And as I glide with the breeze,
I watched the blinding sun pride.
The arms leading me,
To a place I never thought exist,
Over the city I used to live,
Through the sky of vast mysteries.
Unable to blink,
I ventured the world thorough,
With you, the one leading me,
By my side and my company.

75. mirror

Everytime I look at the mirror,
I wonder if I have actually look through the mirror,
Through the window that seperated our world,
Looking out to another me,
To another world that looks similar but not the same.
Where the moon rises in the morning, and the sun is dimly gray.

76. LETTER TO THE LIVING

I want to say that I'm happy,
I want to cheer you up and see you smile,
Want to take pictures together again, and post them all online.
I want to bake your favourite cake, with purple icing; just how
you've like it,
I want to light up the fireworks,
Kiss under the stars as our hands intertwined between.
I want to wake up with you, your eyes, your greetings with your
lips being mine and always.
I want to hug you from behind, kiss your neck as you make our
meal,
Caressing your tummy, where our child has been waiting.
I want to wipe your tears, kiss your worries away, gently put you
to sleep.
I want to be well for you,
So I can keep you company, be there for you when you need me.
I wish we could own time, wish to see our son.. but I have to
leave.

77. LOSS....

Loss, isn't something we can escape from,
It's hurt, it kills.
More even to alter the death;
a dream drive by regrets.

Fate, something that already decided,
It's abstract, it exist.
Fighting it is like facing the sea;
the tornado, the tsunami;
Lost, and dying.

I give up, I surrender.
I won't deny, won't dispute.
Not that it'll do any different,
But, to accept.. I refuse.

78. Personality

Personality is not just a common name, It's responsible for giving u fame. Horoscope doesn't decide your future, Always keep some distance from suture. Going and coming both are life's part, Personality can directly kill the heart. Personality is not just a common name, It's responsible for giving u fame. A suitable glimpse is enough to burn your eyes, This world is very large in size. Personality earns a title of praise, Senile' s phrases are always dipped in blaze. Personality is not just a common name, It's responsible for giving u fame.

79. MY WAY

Writing poems help me cope,
Though some words are wrong and unheard,
Know that it was raw and pure,
Not from mind but my heart's core.
Some might relatable, some can't be understood.
It's what my heart says, the language it spoke.
And I turned them into words of poems;
A melody my heart sings that no pitch could follow through

80. silence...

I'm sorry,
I can't forget you,
My tears and fears are all because of you.
You're the angel, you're the demon,
I can't seem to let you go; my inner pieces.
I tear you apart, and build you back up,
I burn you to death, then let your ash reborn again.
I'm your prosecutor, I'm your saviour.
I love you, but i despise your existence.
Whatever i do, is all solely for your torture.
Every words that i spat, solely for your well-being.
You're the sun, shining so brilliantly,
You're the darkness, where evil roams freely.

May one day, we'll be free
from each other's destiny.

81. THE GOD WHO LOVE YOU

must be troubling for the god who loves you
To ponder how much happier you'd be today
Had you been able to glimpse your many futures.
It must be painful for him to watch you on Friday evenings
Driving home from the office, content with your week—
Three fine houses sold to deserving families—
Knowing as he does exactly what would have happened
Had you gone to your second choice for college,
Knowing the roommate you'd have been allotted
Whose ardent opinions on painting and music
Would have kindled in you a lifelong passion.
A life thirty points above the life you're living
On any scale of satisfaction. And every point
A thorn in the side of the god who loves you.
You don't want that, a large-souled man like you
Who tries to withhold from your wife the day's disappointments
So she can save her empathy for the children.
And would you want this god to compare your wife
With the woman you were destined to meet on the other campus?
It hurts you to think of him ranking the conversation
You'd have enjoyed over there higher in insight
Than the conversation you're used to.
And think how this loving god would feel

Knowing that the man next in line for your wife
Would have pleased her more than you ever will
Even on your best days, when you really try.
Can you sleep at night believing a god like that
Is pacing his cloudy bedroom, harassed by alternatives
You're spared by ignorance? The difference between what is
And what could have been will remain alive for him
Even after you cease existing, after you catch a chill
Running out in the snow for the morning paper,
Losing eleven years that the god who loves you
Will feel compelled to imagine scene by scene
Unless you come to the rescue by imagining him
No wiser than you are, no god at all, only a friend
No closer than the actual friend you made at college,
The one you haven't written in months. Sit down tonight
And write him about the life you can talk about
With a claim to authority, the life you've witnessed,
Which for all you know is the life you've chosen.

BY CAURL DENNIS

82. THE GIRL WHO LIVED

Down and Down they went
Against the slapping of
frigid biting winds,
demoralising sloppy sleet,
heavy overnight iron-gray sky.
Hard legs felt no cuts and bruise.
Dull hands dangled side by side.
Dry mouths with silent submission.
Fierce hair hardly met care.
Lustreless eyes lost sight of beauty.
Minds blanketed with ultra darkness.
Pride and Ego-- vanity they could not afford.
Heart-- where it might be?

No hearts had made their ways now.
For when the loved one
was tortured with insidious weapons
by the infernal creatures
who had also been lost themselves
in the midst of the barbaric operation
led by the Satan's son himself,
each strike of devil on the loved
was also felt by the lover.
To love was to die again and again.

Afraid of loving big things,
Hearts were trained to love small things.
Smaller and Smaller
things they loved,
Harder and Harder
it was to love themselves.

"To breathe, To breathe, To breathe
Until I end one day"
-- became their mantra.
Living dead they were,
No longer human.
Merely docile robots.
Oblivious of the past,
Ignorant of the future.
Neither accepting nor denying
they were a refuse to be burnt,
Nevertheless making their way
into the Gas chamber.

Amongst the nameless numbered prisoners
One woman was singled out
to dance for one Officer.
Dead was she, a long unknown ago.
Swaying her left over arms,
Lifting her weightless feet,
Twirling and twirling round the lane
where memories of her as a dancer

became vivid and vivider.
Alive was she, momentarily
When she danced
Approached him
Seized his gun
Shot him dead.
Exercising her lost freedom
Throwing off her real prison
She was shot dead
Not as an automaton
But as an autonomous being.

83. GOODBYE

Hard like breaking the iceberg,
Last words were heavy to say.
But it's a step on the journey,
On the highway towards home.

Life is like a busy guesthouse,
We are here for a moment,
So if ways come to cross,
Better we encourage each other.

But we're not to stay attached,
Be it a family, friend or best friend,
At a certain point we'll separate,
For in the end w'all become stories.

Don't cry for it'll surely have to be,
Play your hand well today,
That you'll always have smiles,
As you gaze on memories hang in air.

Knowing you're not here forever,
Love people and use things to do so,
The opposite absolutely never works,
And every sawn seed must be reaped.

Sometimes emotions will hit harder,
That conscious will give it a place.
it happens that souls intertwine,
That it's hard to recall why we're here.

But stand on your ground firmly,
Cherish good times you experienced.
Tell a good story from the guesthouse,
For goodbye means God Be with ye.

84. AT THE ELEVEN HOUR

No matter the worst you face in life,
Do not be dismayed.
Failure might have been to you,
Like a pest to the host.
Yet do not be dismayed I say.
For at the eleventh hour,
Your situation will change.

Like a surprise on a birthday,
Unlike the troubles on a doomsday.
Even so, do not be afraid!
For your savior might be near.
To bind you up from your fear,
And totally wipe away every tear.
Right at the eleventh hour.

Like a wrecking vessel; On a stormy sea.
Your sickness may worsen,
And your problems may increase.
Though the pain may seem everlasting.
Yet anticipate for joy unending.
For at the eleventh hour,
Shall your mouth be wide opened;

And your smiles spread abroad.

At the eleventh hour,
Shall your redeemer appear,
Drying out from your face every tear.
And as the sun rise from the East,
So shall your smiles beam through several feasts.
Recovering all your wasted years.
And from your stressed journey to the West;
Would you finally meet your rest.

85. IN THE SHADOW OF YOUR WARM

In the shadow of your warm love
I feel so safe and secure,
And your soft, caring hands
Urge me on to bravely endure.
Your smiles soothe and ease the pain
Of another dark and lonely day;
The rainbow appears amid the rain,
My sorrow as quickly melts away.
A reassuring glow within your eyes
Tells me that you understand
The complicated ways of my sighs
Born of thoughts truly grand.
I continue to look upon your face
And gain a calm heart, my sweet solace.

86. In the beginning

In the beginning.
I was with the face.
The face cracked into coarse pieces.
I could not repair.

In the beginning.
I was with the eyes.
The eyes melted into a flow of tears.
I could not stanch.

In the beginning.
I was with the beauty.
The beauty faded away with the body.
I could not crave.

In the beginning.
I was with the heart.
The heart turned a place of nightmares.
I could not dream.

87. YOU

Beautiful happy girl keeps my mind in pain,
With smile glad of her beauty can't even drain,
She makes my mind run insane,
Someone's daughter reaching to her is in vain,

Its like I'm on cocaine,
Feelings are the ones tied to me in chain,
No idea to explain,
Mind only set to have its own champagne,

I wanna know you; come sun or rain,
Your love be the one running in my veins,
Wanna make you my princess; one and main,
But reaching to you can't attain,

Please hear my cry; make me gain,
Please feel what I feel; make my heart fain,
It's you, only you I wanna entertain,
Be your best for worst even humane.

88. I LOVE YOU

I feel jealous,
I feel weak and lost.
Sometimes it's like my heart sinks in,
I Wanna go away but at the same time, you're all I want.

I know I'm thinking too much,
I know it's nothing like that.
I try to control my emotions,
But I lose every time so bad.

I know you love me,
I know you care for me as well.
I trust you but can't let someone be close to you,
Cause I love you like hell!!

89. I WANT TO

*I want to write what I feel
but my mind is empty.*

*I want to cry out
but my eyes are all dried out.*

*I want to tell you how I feel
but words are dead long ago.*

*I want to let it go
but my heart says to hold on...*

90. A letter to my crush

To the one who had stolen my heart,
At our first glance from the very start,
Exchanging awkward small talks and smiles,
Not realising that it would lead us to a million miles.

So you became a song that I would listen to,
Lyrics were your words of deepest secrets,
And the rhythms described the cries that your mind tried to sing,
Like an endless loop in playlist and ringtone,
I promised to be your music, a support to bring.

Naive and reckless I was when it came to emotions,
Mistaking your kindness as love and affection,
A prince charming in my fairy tales,
A daydream wish to live happily ever after,
But now, it's just pain and nightmares of scattered heart pieces
and shattered dreams.

I loved you,
But you never once did.

91. soulmate

I'm searching for you everywhere.
You must be somewhere out there.
Why are you taking so much time.
Just already come in my life.

I know you'll understand me like no one does
And care for me because
You're the one for me.
You are my soulmate.

92. night questioned

Beautifully the nature is crafted. Divison of life is into rural and urban. U know traditional thing is turban. A cheerful day blossomed,

At the end night questioned. Twinkling stars are distributed, But smart man is not muted.

A cheerful day blossomed, At the end night questioned. It was the journey started, Peace is so much lazy War is everytime crazy. A cheerful day is blossomed, At the end night questioned. Proffesional used to say amature, That they have to be mature. Crucial behaviour earns nothing, By shaina Arora

In the poems 'shaina' says something. A cheerful day is blossomed, At the end night questioned.

93. ROOTS OF MEMORIES

Millions of years back in the past, Some love spreading birds asked.

How the heart and mind is too smart, All the memories are their major part.

When the eyes don't sleep at a time, Roots of memories at that moment slime.

Mind and heart soon makes present blind,

Smile and frown appears on the face with design.

Symptoms of happiness when knocks the mind, Heart becomes at that moment very kind.

A man's whole journey get muted,

When all the memories get uprooted.

94. BERANG RAATEIN

ये बेरंग रातें भी कितिनी हसीन हुआ करती थी

के जब तू मेरे साथ हुआ करती थी,

वो बारिश का मौसम हुआ करता था,

और प्यारी प्यारी बातें हुआ करती थी,

ये बेरंग रातें भी कितिनी हसीन हुआ करती थी

95. DUNIYAA

Le Chal Aisi Duniya Me Mujhko,

Jaha Phool Ho Par Kaante Na Ho,

Dharmo Ke Naam Pe Insan Baate Naa Ho,

Jaha Mohabbat Me Jhuthe Waade Na Ho,

Jaha Sirf Ache Din Ho Buri Raate Na Ho,

Jaha Log Dukh Chupane Ke Liye,

Jhutha Muskurate Na Ho,

Jaha Insan Khud Ko Dusre,

Insan Se Unchaa Btate Naa Ho,

Jaha Paisa Naa Ho Sirf Gyan Ho,

Jaha Mahilao Ka Samman Ho.

Jaha Budhape Ka Na Darr Dikhe,

Na Jawani Ka Abhi Maan Ho,

Le Chal Aisi Duniya Me Mujhko,

Jo Yaha Se Bilkul Anjaan Ho.!!

96. AURAT

AADAR NAHI KADAR NAHI AURAT H KYA KHABAR NAHI,

JO RASTA LAGE SAHI INHE KARE JO MANN KAHI,

KABHI-KABHI NA HAR GHADI HAI BETIYA

KURBAA HUI, MADAD NAHI FARAK NAHI BS SARHADE

FANAH HUI, KARENGE KUCH SOCHENGE KUCH YEH

BOLIYA HAR WAKT RAHI,

KIYA NA KUCH SUJHA NA KUCH BSS BAATE KI BADI-BADI,

HAI JAAN TU JAHAAN TU YE SHABD AAJ HAI ANSUNI,

KAHANIYA SI LAGG RAHI JO BAATE THI KAHI KABHI,

HQA SAHI YA QA NAHI THI SIKHI BAAT JANAM SE HI,

FIR BHOOLE QUH JHOOLE QU IN RAASTO PE

HAR GHADI..!!

97. MOTHER'S WOMB

Darkness and I were identical twins in my mother's womb
I was too weak so I consumed it,
Too weak to withstand it,
It's grown on me,
So I frown on it,
now i can't fight it,
cause it's in me like a part detached from itself
just to find me,
a vengeful soul which never dies,
Which never found key to any planet,
But to stay in my body like a whole universe dealt up in the skies,
You ask me the reason to why I love the sky,
Now you know I always see the other half of me In the air to fill
my eyes.

98. Dear me

How to save myself from someone who
is already stuck inside of me for so long?

Since the day we met,
You'd given me vibes that stole the attention of mine,
Allowing me to chain your image up in my mind,
As so every single moments couldn't be forgotten.

99. A Small Needful Fact

Is that Eric Garner worked
for some time for the Parks and Rec.
Horticultural Department, which means,
perhaps, that with his very large hands,
perhaps, in all likelihood,
he put gently into the earth
some plants which, most likely,
some of them, in all likelihood,
continue to grow, continue
to do what such plants do, like house
and feed small and necessary creatures,
like being pleasant to touch and smell,
like converting sunlight
into food, like making it easier
for us to breathe.

by Ross Gay

100. EK SHAKSH

Ek Shaksh Mujhse Khawabo Me Mulaqate Karta Hai,

Jiske Ek Ishare Par Badal Bhi Barsate Karta Hai,

WORDSBYRISHT Meri Gali Me Ek Khidki Hai Jisse Chand Nikalta Hai,

Wahi Pados Me Ek Shayar Hai Jo Baate Karta Hai,

Teri Maujudgi Hai Teri Khushboo Bhi,

Tera Kajal Bhi Teri Aankhen Padta Hai,

Banjar Zamee'n Bhi Sabz Ho Jati Hai,

Tera Nigah E Karam Jaha Pe Padta Hai,

Sheher Me Teri Khoobsurti Se Wakif Hai Sabhi,

Shaksh Teri Taarif Aate Jaate Karta Hai.!!

Thank You

THANK YOU EVERYONE FOR YOU PRECIOUS TIME AND SUPPORT.

THANKS TO THE EDITOR, PUBLICATION , AND TO ALL TEAM WHO WORK FOR THIS BOOK

SPECIAL THANKS TO WRITER MISS "SHAYNA ARORA" FOR THESE BEAUTIFULL POETRIES WITHOUT THEM IT CAN'T POSSIBLE .

WE REALLY APPRECIATE YOU FOR INKING SUCH BEAUTIFUL THROUGH THE WORDS .

WELL WISHES FOR YOUR BRIGHT FUTURE .WITH LOTS OF LOVE AND GOOD VIBES.